WE WORK AS A TEAM

BY CHARLOTTE TAYLOR

 Gareth Stevens
PUBLISHING

Please visit our website, www.garethstevens.com. For a free color catalog of all our high-quality books, call toll free 1-800-542-2595 or fax 1-877-542-2596.

Cataloging-in-Publication Data
Names: Taylor, Charlotte.
Title: We work as a team / Charlotte Taylor.
Description: New York : Gareth Stevens Publishing, 2021. | Series: We've got character! | Includes glossary and index.
Identifiers: ISBN 9781538256312 (pbk.) | ISBN 9781538256336 (library bound) | ISBN 9781538256329 (6 pack)
Subjects: LCSH: Interpersonal relations–Juvenile literature. | Teamwork (Sports)–Juvenile literature. | Cooperativeness–Juvenile literature. | Group problem solving–Juvenile literature.
Classification: LCC BF723.I646 T39 2021 | DDC 158.2–dc23

Published in 2021 by
Gareth Stevens Publishing
111 East 14th Street, Suite 349
New York, NY 10003

Copyright © 2021 Gareth Stevens Publishing

Designer: Sarah Liddell
Editor: Megan Quick

Photo credits: Cover, p. 1 Robert Kneschke/Shutterstock.com; background throughout Igor Vitkovskiy/Shutterstock.com; p. 5 SDI Productions/E+/Getty Images; pp. 7, 15 Monkey Business Images/Shutterstock.com; p. 9 LightField Studios/Shutterstock.com; p. 11 Richard Lewisohn/DigitalVision/Getty Images; p. 13 Ruslan Huzau/Shutterstock.com; p. 17 RichVintage/iStock/Getty Images Plus/Getty Images; p. 19 FatCamera/iStock/Getty Images Plus/Getty Images; p. 21 kali9/E+/Getty Images.

Printed in the United States of America

Some of the images in this book illustrate individuals who are models. The depictions do not imply actual situations or events.

CPSIA compliance information: Batch #CS20GS: For further information contact Gareth Stevens, New York, New York at 1-800-542-2595.

Find us on

CONTENTS

Boldface words appear in the glossary.

Terrific Teamwork

When you play soccer or baseball, you are part of a team. You work together. You play your best. When you work with others at home or school, you are also part of a team. You work together to reach your **goal**.

Class Helpers

Jordan was working on a hard math problem. She was not sure how to **solve** it. Two members of her class gave her some ideas. They worked through each step of the problem. They solved the problem by working as a team.

Emma's class was holding a bake sale to raise money. They needed to make 200 cookies! Everyone brought **ingredients** to Emma's house. Together, they baked the cookies. It was a big job, but it was easy because they worked as a team.

Pat's class put on a play. Some children wrote the words for the play. Others made the **costumes**. Some children acted or danced in the play. Each person had a job. They worked as a team to put on a great play.

Family Time

Mark's mom had to work late. Mark's older sister did the cooking. Mark and his younger sister put together a salad. When Mark's mom got home, dinner was ready. The whole family had worked as a team.

Good Neighbors

Nicole's neighbor was sick. Nicole and her friends took turns walking his dog and taking care of his plants. Nicole's mom and dad drove him to the doctor. Other neighbors brought him food. Everyone worked as a team to help their neighbor.

Team Play

Drew was playing baseball. He really wanted to pitch. The **coach** put him in left field. It was not as fun as pitching. But Drew knew his job was important. He did not **complain**. Drew played his best to help the team.

Anthony was playing in a basketball game. He had the ball. He could try to make a basket with a long throw. Joe, his **teammate**, was closer to the basket. Anthony passed it to him. Joe made the basket! Anthony was a good team player.

Jess was at bat. Her team was losing the game by one run. Jess struck out and the game ended. Her team did not blame her for the loss. They had all played a part in the game. A team wins or loses together.

GLOSSARY

coach: someone who trains and teaches a player or team

complain: to say or write about being unhappy about something

costume: clothes that someone wears to look like a different person or thing

goal: something someone is trying to do or achieve

ingredient: one of the things that is used to make food

solve: to find a way to deal with a problem

teammate: a person who is on the same team

FOR MORE INFORMATION

BOOKS

Gordon, Jon, and Lauren Gallagher. *The Hard Hat for Kids: A Story About 10 Ways to Be a Great Teammate*. Hoboken, NJ: John Wiley & Sons, 2018.

Johnson, Kristin. *In It Together: A Story of Fairness*. Minneapolis, MN: Millbrook Press, 2018.

WEBSITES

PBS Kids: Teamwork Games
pbskids.org/games/teamwork/
Check out lots of fun games that teach about teamwork.

WonderGrove Kids: Work Together as a Team
www.youtube.com/watch?v=TZqFYtWCWXg
Watch a short video about the importance of working together.

INDEX